remembering
what
this
is

remembering
what
this
is

robert maoz kržišnik

First Printing: 2020
Print on demand

Designer: Lucija Kržišnik
Editor: Graham Timmins

ISBN 978-961-94753-1-7

Publisher:
Robert Maoz Kržišnik, s.p.
Ob dolenjski železnici 12
1000 Ljubljana, Slovenia, EU
www.thatfield.eu

this lifetime is short
let us experience it fully
let us dwell in our true nature
let us meet in our innocence.

preface
who am I?
what am I?
where am I?
when am I?
what is real?
where do we go?
what about others?
so, now what?

Just half a year ago I had no idea whatsoever that I would write this present book, let alone so quickly. Yet after my memoir This Miraculous Life was published in 2019, I soon started to notice two distinct waves surfacing in me. The first was a sense that, after several decades of dedicated work, my inner healing had largely completed and I could finally feel myself to be fully present and embodied in this life. And the second one was a growing awareness that another layer of my being wanted to be brought into this world and to be expressed in writing.

Spontaneously I started to gather together and organise all my personal notes from diverse spiritual experiences over the years, and at some point a language suddenly emerged in me which enabled me to articulate these experiences much more precisely and fully than ever before. The inner clarity of the concepts appeared to have an almost mathematical precision, and yet as I formulated them in words, it seemed like I was writing poetry. It all started to flow through me as if it was my own natural language that I was just remembering.

What followed was a frantic period of typing out this material, which seemed to have been waiting fully formed for an eternity deep within me, ready to be released. Within a month this book was written. Somehow it came to me in English, without much effort or struggle, despite that being my third language.

Of course this little book only represents my current capacity to articulate something which cannot be captured in words. It is like showing you a photo of an elephant, only to hear you protest: "But this is not an elephant! An elephant is much bigger, heavier than this. And it is alive, moving, breathing. And it has a distinct smell. And warmth. This is not an elephant; this is just a silly piece of paper." And you would be right, of course.

So yes, while the images and thoughts and metaphors in this book are only frozen pictures of the flow of life that our minds have no way of fully grasping anyway, they do point at the meta-reality I (and many others) have been perceiving. I am happy to say that they got me a bit further from the point where I had been stuck for a long time, the place St. Augustine described so eloquently in relation to the question of what time was: "If no one asks me, I know what it is. If I wish to explain it to someone, I do not know." This then is my attempt to draw a basic outline map of reality. There will be more precise maps available someday, for certain, yet I hope that in the meantime this one will support both myself and others as we try to orientate ourselves in this life.

When the writing phase was completed, a sense of deep peace and completion descended on me. A sense that I had brought myself into this world more fully than ever before. I was surprised to realize that this book feels way more intimate and personal than my memoir, in which I was already trying to be radically honest about my life. Perhaps because in this book I am revealing myself from the deepest level of my being.

Which, in essence, is exactly what I want to manifest in this life. So, all is good.

I am grateful to my dear Noa for inviting, again and again and again, with a loving smile and sparkling eyes, my heart and soul into this field. I am deeply thankful to my dear daughter Lucija for her infinite trust and appreciation. And then Graham, my editor: you are like a bass player in a rock band; often invisible, yet so crucial.

Robert Maoz Kržišnik,
July 2020

who am I?

This is actually very simple.

You are you.
The one reading these words right now.
Right now.
The one aware of this moment.
This one, you are this very one.

Welcome!

You have always been this very you
ever since you first entered this realm of existence,
and you will always be this very you,
the same you as you are right now.
The indivisible, eternal, unmistakeable, unique you.
Nobody else is you, and you are nobody else.
Yes, this one is you.

Breathing in this very moment,
inhaling and exhaling,
reading, thinking, feeling, being aware.
Right now.
Yes, this one is you.

Welcome into this life.

All is well.

You are welcome into this life.

Right now, in this moment,
you are bringing yourself into this life.
As you have been doing all along.

The more you bring yourself into this dimension of existence,
the more you bring your full nature
through the portal of your body,
into the now, into the here,
the more you are creating space for your unique journey,
for your unique creation.

The more fully you are dancing your dance of life,
your dance of creation,
the more gravity you are creating.

The more you are bending space and time with your gravity,
the more you attract back all the frozen,
traumatized parts of yourself
that have been floating around like space debris on outer orbits,
pulling them back into the warmth, into the light,
letting them melt back into the wholeness of you.

Bringing all of you into this life.

Yes, you are welcome.

In essence, you are not even this 'you' as you know yourself.
You are actually 'that'.

Yet as you bring 'that',
the amorphous flow of life,
through the portal of your body
into the here and now of this space-time continuum,
into this physical universe,
the amorphousness articulates into 'you':
into what you experience as your known self;
into your thoughts, your feelings,
into your-self.

Through the portal of your body
you are ever-becoming the one you know as yourself.
Through the portal of your body
you are welcoming yourself into this experience of existence.

Into this creation.

Into this life.

Welcome.

And perhaps the most important thing to remember:
you are whole as you are
you are already complete.
You are already perfect
and you were never anything less than perfect,
so there is no need to try to make yourself different,
no need to fix yourself.
Ever. At all.

Actually, you cannot fix yourself anyway.
You can change your mind, your body,
you can change the way you relate
- to others, to the world and to yourself -
but yourself, in the very core, you cannot change.

You are already enlightened, in oneness,
as you never stopped being in oneness.
It is actually not even possible to be anything else.
You just forgot it, or, more precisely,
your mind has no way of comprehending it;
and you identify yourself with your mind, so...

Yes, you are already totally free
and this is not a prison to liberate yourself from.
This is a dance floor.

So, welcome,
you perfect, free, eternal you,
welcome into this life.

what am I?

·

Many thoughts can be used in an attempt to capture your nature,
but none of them will ever make it.
Many words can be used in an effort to articulate what you are,
but none of them will ever really describe you in your fulness.
It would be like trying to capture the vastness of an ocean
with a teaspoon.

Your mind cannot even begin to imagine
the beyond-beyond nature of what you are in essence.
It is not even close to having the necessary capacity for that.
All it can do is to create simple images, like, for instance...

...that you are pure Consciousness,
slowly waking up into the world you created.

...or that you are a being of light with amnesia,
now afraid to fully shine.

...or that you are simply one of many points of view,
through which Consciousness is witnessing
the flow of its creation.

...or that you are both the cosmic dancer
and the delighted audience as well.

In absolute terms you are all of it:
the stars and planets, animals and plants, past and future,
you are all of that.

And everybody else is all of that too.

Who you are is completely unique,
yet what you are is exactly the same as everybody else.

Imagine a plant of immeasurable proportions,
growing somewhere behind this universe,
bearing a countless number of fruits.

What you experience as yourself
is a fruit of this plant.
You are this plant,
and you are also a fruit of this plant.

Slowly you are becoming self-aware,
like other fruits are too.

Through these fruits,
Consciousness expands into the field of possibilities,
creating forms of beingness
that represent various possible qualities,
countless patterns of existence
that dance with each other,
creating bigger and more complex designs.

What you experience as yourself is also such a pattern,
a complex combination of possibilities,
as important and unique as every other combination.

In a way you are like a magical torch
throwing light into the darkness.
Yet this torch is not seeking to find what is already there,
but is, with its light, creating the space, the gravitational field.

It is not that you are exploring an already-existing world
in order to inhabit it,
but that you are actually creating the world by observing it,
by bringing your consciousness, your presence into it.

By creating the world you are also creating the experience of time.

Time is not a fixed component of the universe out there.
It is not a pre-set linear movement.
It is a concept, a creation captured within the endless moment.
The whole of time is within this endless moment,
along with all the beginnings, endings, durations...

In a similar way, you are also creating the experience of space.
Things may seem very far or very near.
But actually, nothing is far, as all is within you.
The whole of life is within you.

And you are within the whole of life.

Even your body, your portal into this reality,
is connected with every single particle
in the whole of this universe.

With some practice, with some stillness,
you can remember how to activate the whole of your portal,
the whole of your energy pattern,
and feel the entire universe breathing through your being,
the whole of existence pulsating within your energy field.
Maybe you'd like to try?

Imagine an enormous dragon,
stretched across vastness of the universe.
A cosmic dragon of creation.

It wakes up to create
and then lies down into its creation
to rest
and to witness.

Then it rises up again to create some more,
only to lie down afterwards, exhaling peacefully,
enjoying its creation,
witnessing how it stabilises itself,
cools down, solidifies.

This is the basic heartbeat of creation,
the key rhythm of the cycle of life.

Only that the breathing in and out
is happening simultaneously, not sequentially.
As time itself is also a product of creation.

So the whole of time is inside this single timeless moment,
within which the dragon creates and rests in its creation.

And yes, you are like this dragon,
or, perhaps, we could even say
that you are this dragon.

Just like everybody else is.

You are a work of art.
An incredible ongoing dance, an emerging painting
that the miraculous force of life, Consciousness itself,
has been putting together.
Adding a bit of this here and a bit of that there,
putting you into this current version
of yourself in this moment,
while the dance is already moving you on.

Together with everybody else, you are, right now,
playing the incredibly rich symphony of life.
Each one of us is contributing unique sounds and tones
and together we are creating this cosmic composition,
which ripples endlessly out through space-time.
This is how together we manifest existence.

In this symphony of life
there are intense and peaceful parts,
disturbing and comforting ones,
gentle ones as well as the rough.
All of us together are trying out possible combinations,
composing and playing at the same time
as enjoying and witnessing.

Yes, you are indeed a work of art of cosmic proportions,
showing yourself to the rest of us,
presenting us with your unique dance.

Oh, what a beautiful creation,
whispers the cosmic audience.

Thank you for your beautiful dance.

where am I?

You are in what we can call The Universe.
We can also call it the creation of the experience of existence.
The ongoing formation, happening in the same eternal moment.

It is the creation of the one and the same Consciousness,
experienced and witnessed through billions of points of view.

In a way, it is all energy, moving in various shapes and patterns,
pulsating to the level of the momentary existence of particles,
forming together the frequency that we experience as matter.

Just as pixels on a screen,
pulsating in and out at incredible speeds,
create the impression of landscapes, people, movement,
whole worlds …
so the movement of energy creates
the experience of the physical universe.

Every thought, emotion, vision, sense
is a new and unique pattern of energy.

These patterns meet each other,
interact, give birth to new forms,
which give rise to new movements.

Every one of them is exploring the field of possibilities.

Every movement creates a new world of opportunities.

In every single moment.

Every creation,
be it a movement,
a thought,
a person,
a form of life,
a thing…
is a specific energetic vibration,
with a unique frequency
which needs space-time to complete its move,
to cool down,
to burn out.

Like every tone played on an instrument
needs space-time to ring out and gradually fade away.

Like every movement of a dancer
needs space-time to complete and to transition into the next one.

Like every stroke of the brush
needs space-time to contribute to the perfection of the painting.

In order for creation to be possible,
there needs to be separation.
If there is no separation to create duality,
then there is only oneness:
no time, no space, no matter, no mass, no energy.
No movement whatsoever.
Only static oneness.

The duality, the polarity
opens up the portal into the possibility of creation.
The duality is therefore ultimately essential
and immensely precious,
if there is to be an exploration of possibilities,
if there is to be a creation.

Duality is like a question,
like an inquiry into the field of possibilities
which stimulates manifestation.
It inspires the movement.
It initiates the dance of creation.

And yes, while duality is a question, an inquiry,
it does not seek an answer.
This creation is not a riddle to be solved,
it is a miracle to be experienced.

Imagine a sandy beach
wide and stretching into the horizon,
seemingly endless.
You stand on this sand
thinking what could you build out of it.
This is the unmanifested potential of the beach.

So many things could be built out of this sand.
So many possibilities are present in this sand,
right now, in front of your eyes.
And then you make a choice:
to build a sand castle.

And you start, slowly and patiently
shaping the sand into a castle.
You start interpreting the unmanifested potential
into a specific manifestation,
one of the very many possible ones.

The ever-moving wave of unmanifested potential,
the timeless wave of possibilities
becomes a particle,
a specific creation
in a specific location of space-time.

After you have gone home from that beach,
your creation starts cooling down,
fading out,
until it finally dissolves back into the beach,
adding itself to the pool of possibilities,
waiting to be manifested again in a new form
by another creator.

A magnificent cobra
stretches a third of her body upright,
standing vertically,
still, very still.
Slowly, barely visibly, her head leans back,
eyes focused, mouth wide open.
She is ready.

This is the static, unmanifested potential
about to be interpreted, to be manifested.
When will she strike, how, where, none of this is clear yet.

Then the choice is made,
she becomes a he,
the wave transforms into a particle,
into a specific manifestation of a specific possibility,
into a unique creation.
And the whip of the wave snaps itself into existence,
sending ripples in all directions
to meet other ripples, other patterns,
to create new ones
and find their unique ways of completion.
Sparks are flying into the darkness,
slowly cooling down and dying out,
harmonizing back into the oneness,
waiting for a new in-breath, a new act of creation
through which they will all be gathered
for a new manifestation.

If you are reading this now,
that means that the cobra has made her choice
and has struck.

when am I?

You are now,
of course,
when else could you be?

Yet this now is big,
really, really vast.
It is all-encompassing.
It is eternal.

Actually, there is absolutely nothing
outside of the now.

Now is all the time there is.

The now has a dimension of depth, though.
The deeper you are in the now,
the more you are embracing the experience,
the more you are integrating the existence,
the more you are present to your creation and your witnessing.

Can you just be in the now,
and let yourself sink into it fully?

Time is a concept, a make-believe
that makes it possible for you to witness the creation,
from the inside.
To explore and process it
with the mind that you use in this existence.

Time is not running objectively somewhere outside of you.
It is not measuring something out there.
It is giving you a sense of something within you.

Like when you doze off in your chair
for only a couple of seconds
and you have a dream lasting a couple of weeks.
Now, what was it, seconds or weeks?

Time is the inner experience
which gives you the sense of your inner journey,
capturing the level of its profoundness, its complexity.

And your inner journey is nothing but the process of
creating and witnessing life.
It is the dance of creation that you dance
and through which you create space,
which did not exist before you created it.

By bringing yourself, through the portal of your body,
into this dimension of existence,
you are expanding the space,
and creating the experience of time.

And all of this is happening now.

Time and space are connected,
intertwined,
two sides of the same coin.
They exist and move together.

The creation of time creates space
and the creation of space creates time.
When one of them emerges
it creates a void that pulls the other one in.
We could say that time is flowing into the creation of new space.
It flows into the continuous evolution of it all.

Imagine a fire burning
and producing a small cloud of smoke above it.
The smoke is slowly expanding in all directions.
Bit by bit, it's occupying the space
in which before there was no smoke.
It's expanding its volume.
Creating an ever-bigger cloud.

Now imagine the fire burning is Consciousness
and the smoke is the universe, created by it.
This is how our space-time comes into existence.

Yet, ultimately,
it is all just now.

what is real?

It may seem that there is a radical difference
between what is true reality,
and what is just apparent reality, an illusion, not real,
and that discerning between the two
will have a profound effect on the quality of your existence.

Actually the only difference between the two is
that they are, in essence, two different thoughts,
two different concepts, two different patterns.

Together they create an apparent polarity.

Yet in essence
they are the same.

Everything that exists,
is a creation,
a story,
a game of gods:
therefore an illusion.

And that illusion, that creation, that play
is the only truth,
the only reality
that there is.

So, you can just relax.
It is all good.

There is a story floating in the space between individuals,
a collective narrative,
that this life is some kind of a prison
that you need to break free from.

That this life is a suffering
that you need to liberate yourself from.

That this is some sort of evil illusion that you are caught in,
maya, a grand hallucination
that you have to wake up from.

If you believe in this,
then you will spend this precious lifetime in fear,
seeking salvation through giving away your creative power
to some religion,
some belief system,
some spiritual teacher...

Of course, it IS all an illusion,
but it is an illusion that you came here to create.
It is your dance,
it is your art,
it is your creation.

And being an artist, for example a painter,
painting this beautiful creation,
while saying:
"This is not real, it is just a painting, just an illusion..."
would perhaps not be so much fun.

where do we go?

Where does a dancer go,
when giving freedom to her body
to follow the flow of life?

Where does a musician go,
when he lets his fingers improvise
and articulate the flow of life
as it streams through his consciousness?

Like them we are all evolving,
growing towards an ever-greater sensitivity,
an ever-greater receptivity to the flow of life,
in order to be even more able to fully embody it.

Evolving towards a greater mastery of creation,
and a greater mastery of witnessing
and of enjoying the act of creation.

We are waking up
into this moment, into the now.

We are waking up our full nature
into this universe, into this dimension of existence.

The more we wake up
into sheer presence to this moment,
the more we inhabit the depth and the width of the now.
And the more obvious it gets that
the past and the future are only hallucinations,
images and stories in our minds,
slowly dissipating into the void.

The more we wake up to the very nature of existence,
the more we remember that there is no division,
that we are all one,
one manifestation of the same Consciousness.
In oneness.

The more we become aware of that
the less we will be afraid of each other
and of life itself,
and the more our hearts will smile lovingly
at each other.

And our dance will spiral all across the galaxies.

Waking up is not easy,
as the direction of the waking process is unclear.
It is clear that you are waking up from something,
but where are you waking up to is incomprehensible to your mind.

Going to sleep also does not have a clear direction
that your mind could grasp and move towards.
This is why you basically lay down in the evening and wait
for sleep to happen, for it to take over.

In the same way, waking up from your dreams
does not have a clear direction.

In both cases it is about crossing from one dimension to another,
with the mind from the first dimension
not being able to comprehend the other one.

The only thing that is certain is
that any direction that the mind can think of
is not the right one.

And so, the only way to cross into another dimension,
to wake up from one world into another one,
is to let go of trying to control,
to just let go of the known
and allow the unknown to pull you in.

Just let go.

All is well.

Waking up is always a surprise,
always a disorienting experience,
at least for a moment.
Your mind,
which provided you with your sense of self in one world,
with some sort of orientation,
is suddenly rather obsolete in this new world
in which you have woken up.

What you are experiencing now,
your mind of the previous world
was not even able to imagine.

It was locked in a framework
that prevented it from imagining what else was possible.

Yet now when you cross these boundaries
that you were not even aware of,
you realize that by venturing beyond them
you do not get anything
of what your mind was capable of imagining.

Yet you get so much more.

In the same way, the larger reality, which you forgot about
and cannot remember anymore,
is totally incomprehensible to your current mind.

Therefore one thing is for certain,
that whatever you can possibly imagine with your current mind,
the larger reality is way beyond it.

Perhaps the best word for where this is all going is
that it is in essence about remembering.

Remembering our source,
remembering our nature,
remembering our oneness,
remembering our fulness.

The journey of projection from oneness
through the portal of our bodies,
through the opening of this specific viewpoint,
and into this reality, into this dimension of existence,
into this awareness captured by our minds,
was so confusing, so disorienting
that we have forgotten it all.

And now we are trying to remember,
so that we can fully enjoy creating and witnessing,
so that we can embody and experience
this mystery of existence,
explore the miracle of creation,
and bring heaven and earth together.

what about others?

.

The others
who you meet on your journey of existence:
the mothers and fathers,
sons and daughters,
friends and lovers,
and those who you don't know,
just passing by on the street;
and those who really irritate and annoy you,
and those who frighten you,
all of them,
they are all the same.

Each one of them,
every single one,
is divinity embodied,
Goddess and God incarnated.

Yet who they are is different.
They are not you.
And you are not them.

You are all different viewpoints
of the same Consciousness.

Every one that you meet
is a dancer of Life,
bringing themselves through the portals of their bodies
into this moment,
as fully as they possibly can.
Just like you.

Each one is, in essence, pure innocence embodied,
waking up slowly into this reality,
confused, frightened, disoriented, still half asleep,
trying to figure out what is going on,
trying to make sense out of this.

Can you welcome them into this life?
Can you embrace their innocence,
and invite their curiosity into this moment of existence?

Can you receive them fully,
your sisters and brothers,
in their nakedness?

Can you love them
even when they dance in a way you don't like?
Even when they don't want to dance with you at all,
although you really, really want them to?
Can you still meet them with a loving heart?

Can you whisper gently into their hearts,
again and again and again:
"My dear sister, my dear brother,
I am welcoming you,
the whole of you.
You are welcome into this life."

Witnessing creation
brings meaning to Life.
An artist creating a piece of art
does so simply in order to express a flow of energy,
yet the witness completes its meaning.

Witnessing others means holding a space for them
so that they can continue bringing themselves into this world,
so that they can sing their song,
and dance their dance,
as authentically, creatively, directly as possible,
thus enlarging their presence here
and increasing their gravity.

If you try to change them,
to fix them as if they are broken,
you are interfering with their wave, their movement,
and you are contributing to the space for creation
to close down.

Yet the more your witnessing is holding an open space,
the more you are inviting them to find their voice,
to sing to the fullest,
to explore possibilities
and to find ways to harmonise their creation with the whole.

So, can you see
your child, your partner, your parent, your whoever
as a cosmic dancer, searching for their move,
a painter painting a picture of a universe…?

Can you find a way to dance with them
while still keeping your own balance?

Can you join them, with your unique instrument,
to improvise together a composition of cosmic proportions,
a life-inviting harmony?

Can you, as a moving and evolving wave,
together with another moving and evolving wave,
weave a perfect pattern of Life?

Can you support their beauty
to find its full manifestation,
with a loving smile:
"Dance, beloved sister, beloved brother,
dance your dance,
sing your song…
You are welcome to bring yourself in"?

Can you do that,
not because this is a good, correct thing to do,
but because you are aware that
the dancer and the witness
are both essential and equal partners
in this creation?

so, now what?

A short answer to this question is:
"Whatever you want to create and experience."

Not you as this persona, framed by your mind,
conditioned through traumas, culture, language...,
but the pure, innocent, primal experience of you,
the consciousness as it is just entering
through the portal of your body.

However, there is a secret.
You see, it is not so very important
what is happening in your life,
as that is only the landscape of your journey.
What actually defines your experience of aliveness
is from which space you are choosing to relate to this landscape.

If you choose, again and again,
to lean into the experience, into the landscape of life,
like leaning into a wind that is blowing in your face,
deeply and slowly inhaling every moment of this existence,
with the curiosity of a little child,
celebrating the experience with gratitude,
gently stepping into the mysterious forest,
surrendering to the unknown with an inner smile...
...then this life becomes a miraculous dance
and the question itself melts away.

Waking up into this moment,
this one, this very moment
in which you exist now,
waking up fully into the awareness of existence
and into the experience of it,
you might notice how this moment is getting
deeper and wider.

Relaxing into this ever-deepening dimension
of the now,
with the whole of your body,
you are slowly opening your portal more fully.

Relaxing into this moment
like a surfer being fully present on the ocean wave,
attentive and responsive,
yet relaxed and flowing.

This is when the perhaps confusing and overwhelming experience
of a multitude of thoughts and feelings and values and needs
pulling you in various directions
suddenly becomes
a tranquil stream of life,
within the eternity of the present moment.
Then me and you, here and there, right and wrong,
all melt back into the wholeness…

…and you wake up fully into dancing
this dance of life.

Wanting to know, to figure it out,
is seductive and may even seem important,
yet when you know, or when you think you know,
the creative flow of life stops.

It gets flattened into a pre-set format,
frozen into a static picture,
and stored in a photo album
deep in the archives of your mind.

Yes, now you are certain to be right,
and you are happy believing that you have figured it all out,
yet the magic of life is gone.

And it will return
when you will start listening again,
patiently, attentively, with awe and humility,
with the wholeness of yourself,
to this miraculous experience of life
revealing itself in front of your eyes.

It will be back
when you will slow down your steps
and walk as you would walk through a rainbow-forest
on a distant planet, on which you just landed.
One attentive step at a time.

It will embrace you again
when you start listening and opening up to the unknown.
And you will start reaching outside of your known self,
being touched by previously unknown dimensions and possibilities,
…hmmm, the magic of life…

Keeping the innocent, open, curious attitude to life
is not easy at all,
as your mind will try to serve you
with quite the opposite strategy:
to lock the experience of the flow of life
into a stable, frozen picture of "I know."

Your mind has evolved
in order to make sense out of this experience,
to be able to process it, witness it,
it keeps originating countless unique patterns
in the forms of thoughts and ideas,
articulating what you witness.

However, doing that, to the best of its abilities
and in order to serve you,
it keeps flattening the whole of reality into a single surface,
and it tends to fully take over the realm of possibilities,
to fully dominate the space of creation.
And it does so very, very quickly.

Whilst being grateful for and appreciative of this incredible tool,
it is also helpful to remember
that any picture that your mind serves you on a silver plate
is but a narrow slice of the full reality, of the full creation.

So, while enjoying their colourfulness,
keep in your awareness that such pictures are only that,
captivating images.

Your dear mind will do all it can
to provide you with the illusion
of stability and predictability,
in order to keep you sane.
It will create explanations, personal beliefs,
models of the world.
Yet this life, this creation,
is much, much more than a predictable, controllable little
walk in the park.

If you start believing these models and beliefs,
you are marching into a long war with life,
a war which is likely to end
in frustration, helplessness and pain.

Now, if this is something you wish to experience,
then yes, this is exactly the thing to do.

But if you wish to dance fully in this creation,
if you wish to bathe in the ever-emerging
infinite richness of unexpected possibilities,
then instead of trying to make life predictable,
to control it,
go ahead and learn how to dance with it,
how to flow smoothly on its waves,
without trying to freeze these waves into
fixed, static, safe patterns.

Yes, it is about
breathing, flowing, dancing
and, of course,
creating.

Yes, you were beaten, violated, hurt, disappointed, wounded;
yes, you were traumatised,
and there are scars and wounds all over your energetic field.
Pain, loneliness, fear, heartbreak, helplessness…
Your birth into this world did not happen in a few hours,
it took decades, it seems.

All this is still alive in you now.
As there is nothing but now, remember?

Yet all those beliefs about yourself,
that you don't matter, that you don't deserve love,
all these thoughts and emotions and injuries
are only patterns in this energy field of ours,
they are lenses through which you are experiencing yourself.
They are not you.

Leaves fall from the trees in the autumn
to provide material for more creation in the future.
A cycle of emergence and disappearance,
of birth and death,
of inhaling and exhaling.

Nothing in this universe is eternal,
everything keeps moving and transforming,
like a giant cosmic fountain of creation,
spitting out new forms, new patterns,
so that they can live, shine, sparkle.

Your wounds will also heal and the scabs will fall off.
Actually, they are healing and providing you with
new possibilities for creation
right now.

So, keep in your awareness
that this is about creating a unique masterpiece of your life,
while enjoying the process of creation
in the same eternal moment.

Enjoy dancing and witnessing your own dance,
even as you dance for others;
not in order to meet their expectations,
but to show them how life flows
through the unique portal that is you,
so that they can witness the wonder of creation.

It is about increasing your sensitivity
through the whole of your body into the now,
for all the ripples of creation,
for all other manifestations of existence.

It is about learning anew to move and flow with life,
to respond with curiosity and presence
while being in the wholeness of existence.
To surrender to the flow of life and let it move you,
while relaxing into the multidimensionality of it all.

It is about marvelling at this miraculous life
unfolding in front of your eyes,
right now, in this one and only moment,
with the gratitude and appreciation of a humble painter
witnessing the magnificence emerging through his hand.

It is about fully grounding your feet into this experience of life
while making sure the antenna of your backbone
keeps you connected to the waves of oneness.

It is about smiling lovingly with it all.

And, last but not least,
just a reminder that this is all but a game,
a game of Consciousness, a game of gods
who have lost themselves
in our passionate playing.

So, you are very much invited
by life itself,
by all of us together in oneness,
by Consciousness,
by yourself,
to dance, to dance fully.

Only when you dance fully
will you know that you indeed are a dancer.

Only when you sing your heart into this world
will you be fully alive.

Dance, my sister,
sing, my brother,
let us witness you fully,
let your voice touch our hearts
and remind us of
what
this
all
is.

You are welcome,
you are so very welcome.

·

Manufactured by Amazon.ca
Bolton, ON